Entertainment Directory

BOSTON RESTAURANT GUIDE 2020

RESTAURANTS, BARS & CAFES

★★★★★

The Most Positively Reviewed and Recommended Restaurants in the City

EGP Editorial

BOSTON RESTAURANT GUIDE 2020
Restaurants, Bars & Cafés

© Rose F Jones, 2020
© E.G.P. Editorial, 2020

Printed in USA.

ISBN-13: 9781081249618

Copyright © 2020
All rights reserved.

BOSTON RESTAURANT GUIDE 2020
Restaurants, Bars and Cafés in Boston

This directory is dedicated to Boston Business Owners and Managers who provide the experience that the locals and tourists enjoy. Thanks you very much for all that you do and thank for being the "People Choice".

Thanks to everyone that posts their reviews online and the amazing reviews sites that make our life easier.

The places listed in this book are the most positively reviewed and recommended by locals and travelers from around the world.

Thank you for your time and enjoy the directory that is designed with locals and tourist in mind!

TOP 500
RESTAURANTS
Ranked from #1 to #500

Boston Restaurant Guide / Restaurants, Bars & Cafés

#1
Piperi Mediterranean Grill
Category: Mediterranean
Average price: Under $10
Area: Downtown
Address: One Beacon St
Boston, MA 02108
Phone: (617) 227-7471

#2
Dave's Fresh Pasta
Category: Specialty Food, Sandwiches
Average price: $11-30
Area: Davis Square
Address: 81 Holland St
Somerville, MA 02144
Phone: (617) 623-0867

#3
Roast Beast
Category: Sandwiches, Burgers
Average price: Under $10
Area: Allston/Brighton
Address: 1080 Commonwealth Ave
Boston, MA 02215
Phone: (617) 877-8690

#4
Neptune Oyster
Category: Seafood
Average price: $31-60
Area: North End
Address: 63 Salem St
Boston, MA 02113
Phone: (617) 742-3474

#5
Casa Razdora
Category: Italian, Pizza
Average price: Under $10
Area: Financial District
Address: 115 Water St
Boston, MA 02109
Phone: (617) 338-6700

#6
FoMu
Category: Cafe, Vegan
Average price: Under $10
Area: Allston/Brighton
Address: 481 Cambridge
St Allston, MA 02134
Phone: (617) 903-3276

#7
Zo
Category: Greek
Average price: Under $10
Area: Downtown
Address: 3 Center Plz
Boston, MA 02108
Phone: (617) 901-6017

#8
Menton
Category: French, Italian
Average price: Above $61
Area: Waterfront, South Boston
Address: 354 Congress St
Boston, MA 02210
Phone: (617) 737-0099

#9
Hungry Mother
Category: Southern
Average price: $31-60
Area: Kendall Square/MIT
Address: 233 Cardinal Medeiros Ave
Cambridge, MA 02141
Phone: (617) 499-0090

#10
Giacomo's Ristorante
Category: Restaurant
Average price: $11-30
Area: North End
Address: 355 Hanover St
Boston, MA 02113
Phone: (617) 523-9026

#11
Oleana Restaurant
Category: Mediterranean
Average price: $31-60
Area: Inman Square
Address: 134 Hampshire St
Cambridge, MA 02139
Phone: (617) 661-0505

#12
Guru The Caterer
Category: Indian, Caterer
Average price: Under $10
Area: Teele Square
Address: 1297 Broadway
Somerville, MA 02144
Phone: (617) 718-0078

#13
Ten Tables
Category: American
Average price: $31-60
Area: Jamaica Plain
Address: 597 Centre St
Jamaica Plain, MA 02130
Phone: (617) 524-8810

#14
Sam LaGrassa's
Category: Sandwiches
Average price: $11-30
Area: Downtown
Address: 44 Province St
Boston, MA 02108
Phone: (617) 357-6861

#15
L'Espalier
Category: French
Average price: Above $61
Area: Back Bay
Address: 774 Boylston St
Boston, MA 02199
Phone: (617) 262-3023

#16
Blunch
Category: Breakfast & Brunch, Coffee & Tea
Average price: Under $10
Area: South End
Address: 59 E Springfield St
Boston, MA 02118
Phone: (617) 247-8100

#17
El Pelón Taqueria
Category: Mexican, Gluten-Free
Average price: Under $10
Area: Fenway
Address: 92 Peterborough St
Boston, MA 02215
Phone: (617) 262-9090

#18
Taqueria Jalisco
Category: Mexican
Average price: Under $10
Area: East Boston
Address: 291 Bennington St
Boston, MA 02128
Phone: (617) 567-6367

#19
Toro
Category: Tapas Bar
Average price: $31-60
Area: South End
Address: 1704 Washington St
Boston, MA 02118
Phone: (617) 536-4300

#20
Ariana
Category: Afghan, Vegetarian
Average price: $11-30
Area: Allston/Brighton
Address: 129 Brighton Ave
Boston, MA 02134
Phone: (617) 208-8072

#21
Cocobeet
Category: Juice Bar & Smoothies, Sandwiches
Average price: $31-60
Area: Downtown
Address: 100 City Hall Plz
Boston, MA 02108
Phone: (857) 263-8598

#22
Salts Restaurant
Category: French, American
Average price: Above $61
Area: Kendall Square/MIT
Address: 798 Main St Cambridge, MA 02139
Phone: (617) 876-8444

#23
Life Alive
Category: Vegetarian, Vegan
Average price: $11-30
Area: Central Square
Address: 765 Mass Ave
Cambridge, MA 02139
Phone: (617) 354-5433

#24
Galleria Umberto
Category: Pizza, Salad
Average price: Under $10
Area: North End
Address: 289 Hanover St
Boston, MA 02113
Phone: (617) 227-5709

#25
The Capital Grille
Category: Steakhouse, American
Average price: Above $61
Area: Back Bay
Address: 900 Boylston St
Boston, MA 02115
Phone: (617) 262-8900

#26
Blackstrap BBQ
Category: Barbeque
Average price: $11-30
Area: Winthrop
Address: 47 Woodside Ave
Winthrop, MA 02152
Phone: (617) 207-1783

#27
Avana Sushi
Category: Japanese, Sushi Bar
Average price: Under $10
Area: Chinatown
Address: 42 Beach St
Boston, MA 02111
Phone: (617) 818-7782

#28
Rino's Place
Category: Italian
Average price: $11-30
Area: East Boston
Address: 258 Saratoga St
Boston, MA 02128
Phone: (617) 567-7412

#29
Al's State Street Cafe
Category: Sandwiches, Salad
Average price: Under $10
Area: Financial District
Address: 110 State St
Boston, MA 02109
Phone: (617) 720-5555

#30
Atlantic Fish Company
Category: Seafood, Pub
Average price: $31-60
Area: Back Bay
Address: 761 Boylston St
Boston, MA 02116
Phone: (617) 267-4000

#31
Café Mami
Category: Japanese
Average price: Under $10
Area: Porter Square
Address: 1815 Massachusetts Ave
Cambridge, MA 02140
Phone: (617) 547-9130

#32
No. 9 Park
Category: French, Italian
Average price: Above $61
Area: Downtown
Address: 9 Park St
Boston, MA 02108
Phone: (617) 742-9991

#33
Mistral Restaurant
Category: American
Average price: Above $61
Area: Back Bay
Address: 223 Columbus Ave
Boston, MA 02116
Phone: (617) 867-9300

#34
Banh Mi Ngon
Category: Vietnamese, Sandwiches
Average price: Under $10
Area: West Roxbury Center, West Roxbury
Address: 1759 Centre St.
Boston, MA 02132
Phone: (617) 325-0946

#35
Drink
Category: Lounge, American
Average price: $31-60
Area: Waterfront, South Boston
Address: 348 Congress St
Boston, MA 02228
Phone: (617) 695-1806

#36
KO Catering and Pies
Category: Food Stands, Breakfast & Brunch
Average price: Under $10
Area: South Boston
Address: 87 A St
Boston, MA 02127
Phone: (617) 269-4500

#37
Mrs. Jones
Category: Soul Food, Southern
Average price: Under $10
Area: Dorchester
Address: 2255 Dorchester Ave
Dorchester, MA 02124
Phone: (617) 696-0180

#38
Amsterdam Falafelshop
Category: Middle Eastern, Falafel
Average price: Under $10
Area: Davis Square
Address: 248 Elm St Somerville, MA 02144
Phone: (617) 764-3334

#39
Regina Pizzeria
Category: Pizza, Italian
Average price: $11-30
Area: North End
Address: 11 1/2 Thacher St
Boston, MA 02113
Phone: (617) 227-0765

#40
The Druid
Category: Pub, Irish
Average price: $11-30
Area: Inman Square
Address: 1357 Cambridge St
Cambridge, MA 02139
Phone: (617) 497-0965

#41
The Haven
Category: GastroPub, Scottish
Average price: $11-30
Area: Jamaica Plain
Address: 2 Perkins St Jamaica Plain, MA 02130
Phone: (617) 524-2836

#42
Deep Ellum
Category: Pub, American
Average price: $11-30
Area: Allston/Brighton
Address: 477 Cambridge St
Allston, MA 02134
Phone: (617) 787-2337

#43
Canto 6
Category: Bakeries, Coffee & Tea
Average price: Under $10
Area: Jamaica Plain
Address: 3346 Washington St
Jamaica Plain, MA 02130
Phone: (617) 983-8688

#44
The Helmand
Category: Afghan
Average price: $11-30
Area: East Cambridge, Kendall Square/MIT
Address: 143 1st St Cambridge, MA 02142
Phone: (617) 492-4646

#45
Falafel King
Category: Falafel
Average price: Under $10
Area: Beacon Hill
Address: 48 Winter St
Boston, MA 02108
Phone: (617) 338-8355

#46
Flour Bakery + Café Central Square
Category: Coffee & Tea, Bakeries
Average price: $11-30
Area: Kendall Square/MIT
Address: 190 Massachusetts Ave
Cambridge, MA 02139
Phone: (617) 225-2525

#47
Asta
Category: American
Average price: Above $61
Area: Back Bay
Address: 47 Massachusetts Ave
Boston, MA 02115
Phone: (617) 585-9575

#48
Giulia
Category: Italian
Average price: $31-60
Area: Porter Square
Address: 1682 Massachusetts Ave
Cambridge, MA 02138
Phone: (617) 441-2800

#49
The Shawarma Place
Category: Fast Food, Middle Eastern
Average price: Under $10
Area: Davis Square
Address: 201 Elm St Somerville, MA 02144
Phone: (617) 666-9000

#50
Cafe Polonia
Category: Polish, Austrian
Average price: $11-30
Area: South Boston
Address: 611 Dorchester Ave
Boston, MA 02127
Phone: (617) 269-0110

#51
Carlo's Cucina Italiana
Category: Italian
Average price: $11-30
Area: Allston/Brighton
Address: 131 Brighton Ave
Allston, MA 02134
Phone: (617) 254-9759

#52
Punjab Palace
Category: Indian
Average price: $11-30
Area: Allston/Brighton
Address: 109 Brighton Ave
Allston, MA 02134
Phone: (617) 254-1500

#53
Shabu-Zen
Category: Japanese, Chinese
Average price: $11-30
Area: Chinatown
Address: 16 Tyler St
Boston, MA 02111
Phone: (617) 292-8828

#54
Cutty's
Category: Coffee & Tea, Sandwiches
Average price: Under $10
Area: Brookline Village
Address: 284 Washington St
Brookline, MA 02445
Phone: (617) 505-1844

#55
East Side Bar & Grille
Category: Italian
Average price: $11-30
Area: East Cambridge
Address: 561 Cambridge St
Cambridge, MA 02141
Phone: (617) 661-3278

#56
Fish Market Sushi Bar
Category: Sushi Bar, Japanese
Average price: $11-30
Area: Allston/Brighton
Address: 170 Brighton Ave Allston, MA 02134
Phone: (617) 783-1268

#57
Deuxave
Category: American
Average price: Above $61
Area: Back Bay
Address: 371 Commonwealth Ave
Boston, MA 02115
Phone: (617) 517-5915

#58
Ernesto's
Category: Pizza, Desserts
Average price: Under $10
Area: North End
Address: 69 Salem St
Boston, MA 02113
Phone: (617) 523-1373

#59
D'Amelios Off the Boat Italian & Seafood Restaurant
Category: Seafood, Italian
Average price: $11-30
Area: East Boston
Address: 26 Porter St East
Boston, MA 02128
Phone: (617) 561-8800

#60
Cuchi Cuchi
Category: Tapas/Small Plates
Average price: $31-60
Area: Kendall Square/MIT
Address: 795 Main St Cambridge, MA 02139
Phone: (617) 864-2929

#61
Sorellina
Category: Italian
Average price: Above $61
Area: Back Bay
Address: 1 Huntington Ave
Boston, MA 02116
Phone: (617) 412-4600

#62
Café Luna
Category: Coffee & Tea, Sandwiches
Average price: $11-30
Area: Central Square
Address: 403 Massachusetts Ave
Cambridge, MA 02139
Phone: (617) 576-3400

#63
Toraya
Category: Sushi Bar, Japanese
Average price: $11-30
Area: Arlington Center
Address: 890 Massachusetts Ave
Arlington, MA 02476
Phone: (781) 641-7477

#64
James Hook & Co
Category: Seafood
Average price: $11-30
Area: Waterfront, South Boston
Address: 440 Atlantic Ave
Boston, MA 02111
Phone: (617) 423-5501

#65
Garlic 'n Lemons
Category: Middle Eastern, Mediterranean
Average price: Under $10
Area: Allston/Brighton
Address: 133 Harvard Ave Allston, MA 02134
Phone: (617) 783-8100

#66
Pomodoro
Category: Italian
Average price: $31-60
Area: North End
Address: 319 Hanover St
Boston, MA 02113
Phone: (617) 367-4348

#67
Navy Yard Bistro & Wine Bar
Category: Wine Bar, American
Average price: $31-60
Area: Charlestown
Address: 6th St Charlestown, MA 02129
Phone: (617) 242-0036

#68
The Daily Catch
Category: Italian, Seafood
Average price: $11-30
Area: North End
Address: 323 Hanover St
Boston, MA 02113
Phone: (617) 523-8567

#69
Cafe Hemshin
Category: Cafe, Turkish
Average price: Under $10
Area: Downtown
Address: 8 City Hall Ave
Boston, MA 02108
Phone: (617) 227-0505

#70
Pinocchios Pizza & Subs
Category: Pizza, Salad
Average price: Under $10
Area: Harvard Square
Address: 74 Winthrop St
Cambridge, MA 02138
Phone: (617) 876-4897

#71
The Five Seventy Market
Category: Grocery, Juice Bar & Smoothies
Average price: $11-30
Area: South End
Address: 570 Tremont St
Boston, MA 02118
Phone: (857) 362-7525

#72
In House Café
Category: Coffee & Tea, Cafe
Average price: Under $10
Area: Allston/Brighton
Address: 194 Harvard Ave
Allston, MA 02134
Phone: (617) 686-3350

#73
Santarpio's Pizza
Category: Pizza
Average price: Under $10
Area: East Boston
Address: 111 Chelsea St
Boston, MA 02128
Phone: (617) 567-9871

#74
Armando's Pizza & Subs
Category: Pizza, Sandwiches
Average price: Under $10
Area: Huron Village
Address: 163 Huron Ave
Cambridge, MA 02138
Phone: (617) 354-8275

#75
Hamersley's Bistro
Category: American
Average price: $31-60
Area: South End
Address: 553 Tremont St
Boston, MA 02116
Phone: (617) 423-2700

#76
Mi Pueblito Restaurant
Category: Mexican, Latin American
Average price: $11-30
Area: East Boston
Address: 333 Border St
Boston, MA 02128
Phone: (617) 569-3787

#77
Picco
Category: Pizza, Italian
Average price: $11-30
Area: South End
Address: 513 Tremont St
Boston, MA 02116
Phone: (617) 927-0066

#78
Kaze Shabu Shabu
Category: Japanese
Average price: $11-30
Area: Chinatown
Address: 1 Harrison Ave
Boston, MA 02111
Phone: (617) 338-8283

#79
Greek Corner Restaurant
Category: Greek, Mediterranean
Average price: $11-30
Area: North Cambridge
Address: 2366 Massachusetts Ave
Cambridge, MA 02140
Phone: (617) 661-5655

#80
Orinoco
Category: Latin American, Caribbean
Average price: $11-30
Area: South End
Address: 477 Shawmut Ave
Boston, MA 02118
Phone: (617) 369-7075

#81
Tupelo
Category: Southern, Cajun/Creole
Average price: $11-30
Area: Inman Square
Address: 1193 Cambridge St
Cambridge, MA 02139
Phone: (617) 868-0004

#82
KO Pies at the Shipyard
Category: American
Average price: Under $10
Area: East Boston
Address: 256 Marginal St
Boston, MA 02128
Phone: (617) 418-5234

#83
Root
Category: Vegan, Vegetarian
Average price: $11-30
Area: Allston/Brighton
Address: 487 Cambridge St Allston, MA 02134
Phone: (617) 208-6091

#84
True Bistro
Category: Vegan, Vegetarian
Average price: $11-30
Area: Teele Square
Address: 1153 Broadway
Somerville, MA 02144
Phone: (617) 627-9000

#85
Trattoria Toscana
Category: Italian
Average price: $11-30
Area: Fenway
Address: 130 Jersey St
Boston, MA 02215
Phone: (617) 247-9508

#86
Swish Shabu
Category: Japanese, Sushi Bar
Average price: $11-30
Area: Fenway
Address: 84 86 Peterborough St
Boston, MA 02215
Phone: (617) 236-0255

#87
Cafe Rossetti's
Category: Italian
Average price: $11-30
Area: Winthrop
Address: 115 Winthrop Shore Dr
Winthrop, MA 02152
Phone: (617) 539-9990

#88
City Girl Café
Category: Italian, Breakfast & Brunch
Average price: $11-30
Area: Inman Square
Address: 204 Hampshire St
Cambridge, MA 02139
Phone: (617) 864-2809

#89
Grotto
Category: Italian
Average price: $31-60
Area: Downtown, Beacon Hill
Address: 37 Bowdoin St
Boston, MA 02114
Phone: (617) 227-3434

#90
Toscano Restaurant
Category: Italian
Average price: $31-60
Area: Beacon Hill
Address: 47 Charles St
Boston, MA 02114
Phone: (617) 723-4090

#91
Fogo de Chao Boston
Category: Brazilian, Steakhouse
Average price: $31-60
Area: Back Bay
Address: 200 Dartmouth Street
Boston, MA 02116
Phone: (617) 585-6300

#92
Taranta Cucina Meridionale
Category: Latin American, Italian
Average price: $31-60
Area: North End
Address: 210 Hanover St
Boston, MA 02113
Phone: (617) 720-0052

#93
Garden at the Cellar
Category: Pub, American
Average price: $11-30
Area: Central Square
Address: 991 Massachusetts Ave
Cambridge, MA 02138
Phone: (617) 475-0045

#94
Mamma Maria
Category: Italian
Average price: $31-60
Area: North End
Address: 3 N Square
Boston, MA 02113
Phone: (617) 523-0077

#95
S & I Thai
Category: Thai
Average price: Under $10
Area: Allston/Brighton
Address: 168 Brighton Ave
Allston, MA 02134
Phone: (617) 254-8488

#96
Delfino Restaurant
Category: Italian
Average price: $11-30
Area: Roslindale Village, Roslindale
Address: 754 South St Roslindale, MA 02131
Phone: (617) 327-8359

#97
Las Ventas
Category: Spanish, Sandwiches
Average price: Under $10
Area: South End
Address: 700 Harrison Ave
Boston, MA 02118
Phone: (617) 266-0443

#98
Blue Ribbon BBQ
Category: Barbeque
Average price: $11-30
Area: Arlington Center
Address: 908 Massachusetts Ave
Arlington, MA 02476
Phone: (781) 648-7427

#99
Lambert's Rainbow Fruit
Category: Fruits & Veggies, Deli
Average price: Under $10
Area: Dorchester
Address: 777 Morrissey Blvd
Dorchester, MA 02122
Phone: (617) 436-2997

#100
Meridian Food Market
Category: Specialty Food, Sandwiches
Average price: Under $10
Area: East Boston
Address: 121 Meridian St East
Boston, MA 02128
Phone: (617) 567-9725

#101
Union Bar and Grille
Category: American
Average price: $31-60
Area: South End
Address: 1357 Washington St
Boston, MA 02118
Phone: (617) 423-0555

#102
Equal Exchange Café
Category: Coffee & Tea, Sandwiches
Average price: Under $10
Area: North End
Address: 226 Causeway St
Boston, MA 02114
Phone: (617) 372-8777

#103
Al's South Street Cafe
Category: Sandwiches
Average price: Under $10
Area: Waterfront, Leather District, South Boston
Address: 179 Essex St
Boston, MA 02111
Phone: (617) 330-1002

#104
Sunset Grill & Tap
Category: Bar, American
Average price: $11-30
Area: Allston/Brighton
Address: 130 Brighton Ave
Allston, MA 02134
Phone: (617) 254-1331

#105
Lineage
Category: American
Average price: $31-60
Area: Coolidge Corner
Address: 242 Harvard St
Brookline, MA 02446
Phone: (617) 232-0065

#106
Pauli's
Category: Sandwiches, Caterer
Average price: Under $10
Area: North End
Address: 65 Salem St
Boston, MA 02113
Phone: (857) 284-7064

#107
Court House Seafood Restaurant
Category: Seafood Market, Seafood
Average price: $11-30
Area: East Cambridge
Address: 498 Cambridge St
Cambridge, MA 02141
Phone: (617) 491-1213

#108
East Coast Grill
Category: Barbeque, Seafood
Average price: $11-30
Area: Inman Square
Address: 1271 Cambridge St
Cambridge, MA 02139
Phone: (617) 491-6568

#109
Da Vinci Ristorante
Category: Italian
Average price: $31-60
Area: Back Bay
Address: 162 Columbus Ave
Boston, MA 02116
Phone: (617) 350-0007

#110
Flour Bakery + Café
Category: American, Coffee & Tea
Average price: $11-30
Area: Back Bay
Address: 131 Clarendon St
Boston, MA 02116
Phone: (617) 437-7700

#111
My Diner
Category: Diner, Breakfast & Brunch
Average price: Under $10
Area: South Boston
Address: 98 A St
Boston, MA 02127
Phone: (617) 268-9889

#112
Pho Viet's
Category: Vietnamese
Average price: Under $10
Area: Allston/Brighton
Address: 1095 Commonwealth Ave
Boston, MA 02228
Phone: (617) 562-8828

#113
Billy's Sub Shop
Category: Diner, Sandwiches
Average price: Under $10
Area: South End
Address: 57 Berkeley St
Boston, MA 02116
Phone: (617) 426-1822

#114
Giacomo's
Category: Italian
Average price: $11-30
Area: Back Bay
Address: 431 Columbus Ave
Boston, MA 02116
Phone: (617) 536-5723

#115
Michael's Deli
Category: Deli, Caterer
Average price: Under $10
Area: Coolidge Corner
Address: 256 Harvard St
Brookline, MA 02446
Phone: (617) 738-3354

#116
Veggie Galaxy
Category: Vegetarian, Diner
Average price: $11-30
Area: Central Square
Address: 450 Massachusetts Ave
Cambridge, MA 02139
Phone: (617) 497-1513

#117
Andre's Cafe
Category: American
Average price: Under $10
Area: South End
Address: 811 Harrison Ave
Boston, MA 02118
Phone: (617) 267-9599

#118
Franklin Café
Category: Lounge, American
Average price: $11-30
Area: South End
Address: 278 Shawmut Ave
Boston, MA 02118
Phone: (617) 350-0010

#119
Tres Gatos
Category: Tapas Bar, American
Average price: $11-30
Area: Jamaica Plain
Address: 470 Centre St
Jamaica Plain, MA 02130
Phone: (617) 477-4851

#120
Shojo
Category: Chinese, Asian Fusion
Average price: $11-30
Area: Chinatown
Address: 9A Tyler St
Boston, MA 02111
Phone: (617) 423-7888

#121
OTTO
Category: Pizza
Average price: Under $10
Area: Harvard Square
Address: 1432 Mass Ave
Cambridge, MA 02138
Phone: (617) 499-3352

#122
Brown Sugar Cafe
Category: Thai
Average price: $11-30
Area: Allston/Brighton
Address: 1033 Commonwealth Ave
Boston, MA 02215
Phone: (617) 787-4242

#123
Corner Tavern
Category: Bar, American
Average price: $11-30
Area: Back Bay
Address: 421 Marlborough St
Boston, MA 02115
Phone: (617) 262-5555

#124
Emma's Pizza
Category: Pizza
Average price: $11-30
Area: Kendall Square/MIT
Address: 40 Hampshire St
Cambridge, MA 02139
Phone: (617) 864-8534

#125
Green Street
Category: Lounge, American
Average price: $11-30
Area: Central Square
Address: 280 Green St
Cambridge, MA 02139
Phone: (617) 876-1655

#126
Chacarero
Category: Sandwiches, Salad
Average price: Under $10
Area: Downtown
Address: 101 Arch St
Boston, MA 02108
Phone: (617) 542-0392

#127
Cafe Gigu
Category: Cafe, Wine Bar
Average price: $11-30
Area: East Boston
Address: 102 Meridian St
Boston, MA 02128
Phone: (617) 561-4448

#128
Flatbread Company
Category: Pizza
Average price: $11-30
Area: Davis Square
Address: 45 Day St Somerville, MA 02144
Phone: (617) 776-0552

#129
Sullivan's
Category: Fast Food, Burgers
Average price: Under $10
Area: South Boston
Address: 2080 Day Blvd
Boston, MA 02127
Phone: (617) 268-5685

#130
Bom Cafe
Category: Brazilian, Cafe
Average price: Under $10
Area: Inman Square
Address: 1093 Cambridge St
Cambridge, MA 02139
Phone: (617) 864-0395

#131
Sacco's Bowl Haven
Category: Bowling, Pizza
Average price: $11-30
Area: Davis Square
Address: 45 Day St Somerville, MA 02144
Phone: (617) 776-0552

#132
Taste of India Shanti
Category: Indian, Bangladeshi
Average price: $11-30
Area: Dorchester
Address: 1111 Dorchester Ave
Dorchester, MA 02125
Phone: (617) 929-3900

#133
Newtowne Grille
Category: Pizza, Pub
Average price: Under $10
Area: Porter Square
Address: 1945 Massachusetts Ave
Cambridge, MA 02140
Phone: (617) 661-0706

#134
Angela's Cafe
Category: Mexican
Average price: $11-30
Area: East Boston
Address: 131 Lexington St
Boston, MA 02128
Phone: (617) 567-4972

#135
Istanbul'lu
Category: Turkish, Wine Bar
Average price: $11-30
Area: Teele Square
Address: 237 Holland St
Somerville, MA 02144
Phone: (617) 440-7387

#136
B & G Oysters
Category: Seafood, Italian
Average price: $31-60
Area: South End
Address: 550 Tremont St
Boston, MA 02116
Phone: (617) 423-0550

#137
Rod Dee Thai 2
Category: Thai
Average price: Under $10
Area: Fenway
Address: 94 Peterborough St
Boston, MA 02215
Phone: (617) 859-0969

#138
PARK Restaurant & Bar
Category: American, Bar
Average price: $11-30
Area: Harvard Square
Address: 59 JFK St
Cambridge, MA 02138
Phone: (617) 491-9851

#139
Marliave
Category: French,
Average price: $31-60
Area: Downtown
Address: 10 Bosworth St
Boston, MA 02108
Phone: (617) 422-0004

#140
Roy's Cold Cuts
Category: Deli, Pizza
Average price: Under $10
Area: East Boston
Address: 198 Marion St
Boston, MA 02128
Phone: (617) 567-9760

#141
Coppa
Category: Italian, Tapas/Small Plates
Average price: $31-60
Area: South End
Address: 253 Shawmut Ave
Boston, MA 02118
Phone: (617) 391-0902

#142
Sportello
Category: Italian
Average price: $31-60
Area: Waterfront, South Boston
Address: 348 Congress St
Boston, MA 02210
Phone: (617) 737-1234

#143
Gaslight Brasserie Du Coin
Category: French
Average price: $11-30
Area: South End
Address: 560 Harrison Ave
Boston, MA 02228
Phone: (617) 422-0224

#144
Ruth's Chris Steak House
Category: Steakhouse, Seafood
Average price: Above $61
Area: Downtown
Address: 45 School St
Boston, MA 02108
Phone: (617) 742-8401

#145
Posto
Category: Italian, Pizza
Average price: $11-30
Area: Davis Square
Address: 187 Elm St Somerville, MA 02144
Phone: (617) 625-0600

#146
Prezza
Category: Italian
Average price: $31-60
Area: North End
Address: 24 Fleet St
Boston, MA 02113
Phone: (617) 227-1577

#147
Veggie Planet
Category: Vegetarian, Pizza
Average price: Under $10
Area: Harvard Square
Address: 47 Palmer St
Cambridge, MA 02138
Phone: (617) 661-1513

#148
Chicken & Rice Guys Catering & Food Truck
Category: Chicken Wings, Food Truck
Average price: Under $10
Area: Downtown
Address: 5 Childs Rd, Lexington
Boston, MA 02116
Phone: (617) 903-8538

#149
The Village Kitchen
Category: Italian, Pizza
Average price: Under $10
Area: Huron Village
Address: 359 Huron Ave
Cambridge, MA 02138
Phone: (617) 491-3133

#150
Alden & Harlow
Category: American, Breakfast & Brunch
Average price: $31-60
Area: Harvard Square
Address: 40 Brattle St
Cambridge, MA 02138
Phone: (617) 864-2100

#151
Blue Nile Restaurant
Category: Ethiopian
Average price: $11-30
Area: Jamaica Plain
Address: 389 Centre St
Boston, MA 02130
Phone: (617) 522-6453

#152
Deli-icious
Category: Deli
Average price: Under $10
Area: Davis Square
Address: 20 College Ave
Somerville, MA 02144
Phone: (617) 629-4444

#153
FuGaKyu
Category: Sushi Bar, Japanese
Average price: $31-60
Area: Coolidge Corner
Address: 1280 Beacon St
Brookline, MA 02446
Phone: (617) 734-1268

#154
Russell House Tavern
Category: GastroPub, American
Average price: $11-30
Area: Harvard Square
Address: 14 JFK St Cambridge, MA 02138
Phone: (617) 500-3055

#155
West Bridge
Category: Bar, American
Average price: $31-60
Area: Kendall Square/MIT
Address: 1 Kendall Sq
Cambridge, MA 02141
Phone: (617) 945-0221

#156
Delux Café
Category: Bar, American
Average price: $11-30
Area: South End
Address: 100 Chandler St
Boston, MA 02116
Phone: (617) 338-5258

#157
Lone Star Taco Bar
Category: Mexican
Average price: $11-30
Area: Allston/Brighton
Address: 477 Cambridge St
Allston, MA 02134
Phone: (617) 782-8226

#158
Za
Category: Pizza, Salad
Average price: $11-30
Area: East Arlington
Address: 138 Massachusetts Ave
Arlington, MA 02474
Phone: (781) 316-2334

#159
PS Gourmet Coffee
Category: Coffee & Tea, Deli
Average price: Under $10
Area: South Boston
Address: 106 Dorchester St
Boston, MA 02127
Phone: (617) 269-4020

#160
Myers & Chang
Category: Asian Fusion, Gluten-Free
Average price: $11-30
Area: South End
Address: 1145 Washington St
Boston, MA 02118
Phone: (617) 542-5200

#161
Oishii Boston
Category: Sushi Bar, Japanese
Average price: Above $61
Area: South End
Address: 1166 Washington St
Boston, MA 02118
Phone: (617) 482-8868

#162
Lizard Lounge
Category: Music Venue, Burgers
Average price: $11-30
Area: Porter Square
Address: 1667 Massachusetts Ave
Cambridge, MA 02138
Phone: (617) 547-0759

#163
All Star Sandwich Bar
Category: Sandwiches
Average price: $11-30
Area: Inman Square
Address: 1245 Cambridge St
Cambridge, MA 02139
Phone: (617) 868-3065

#164
The Plough & Stars
Category: Music Venue, American
Average price: $11-30
Area: Central Square
Address: 912 Massachusetts Ave
Cambridge, MA 02139
Phone: (617) 576-0032

#165
Fleming's Prime
Steakhouse & Wine Bar
Category: Wine Bar, Steakhouse
Average price: $31-60
Area: Back Bay
Address: 217 Stuart St
Boston, MA 02116
Phone: (617) 292-0808

#166
Silvertone
Category: Italian, GastroPub
Average price: $11-30
Area: Downtown
Address: 69 Bromfield St
Boston, MA 02108
Phone: (617) 338-7887

#167
Kaju Tofu House
Category: Korean
Average price: $11-30
Area: Allston/Brighton
Address: 58 Harvard Ave
Allston, MA 02134
Phone: (617) 208-8540

#168
2nd Street Cafe
Category: Sandwiches, Cafe
Average price: Under $10
Area: East Cambridge
Address: 89 2nd St
Cambridge, MA 02141
Phone: (617) 661-1311

Boston Restaurant Guide / Restaurants, Bars & Cafés

#169
Harvard Faculty Club
Category: Venue & Event Space, American
Average price: Above $61
Area: Harvard Square
Address: 20 Quincy St Cambridge, MA 02138
Phone: (617) 495-5758

#170
The Salty Pig
Category: American
Average price: $11-30
Area: Back Bay
Address: 130 Dartmouth St
Boston, MA 02116
Phone: (617) 536-6200

#171
Jm Curley
Category: American, Lounge
Average price: $11-30
Area: Downtown
Address: 21 Temple Pl
Boston, MA 02111
Phone: (617) 338-5333

#172
The Squeaky Beaker
Category: Cafe, Comfort Food
Average price: $11-30
Area: East Cambridge, Kendall Square/MIT
Address: 675 W Kendall St
Cambridge, MA 02142
Phone: (617) 679-0108

#173
Crema Cafe
Category: Coffee & Tea, Cafe
Average price: $11-30
Area: Harvard Square
Address: 27 Brattle St
Cambridge, MA 02138
Phone: (617) 876-2700

#174
Aquitaine
Category: French
Average price: $31-60
Area: South End
Address: 569 Tremont St
Boston, MA 02118
Phone: (617) 424-8577

#175
The Parish Cafe
Category: Sandwiches, Desserts
Average price: $11-30
Area: Back Bay
Address: 361 Boylston St
Boston, MA 02116
Phone: (617) 247-4777

#176
La Siesta
Category: Mexican
Average price: $11-30
Area: Winthrop
Address: 70-74 Woodside Ave
Winthrop, MA 02152
Phone: (617) 846-2300

#177
Al Dente Restaurant
Category: Italian, Bakeries
Average price: $11-30
Area: North End
Address: 109 Salem St
Boston, MA 02113
Phone: (617) 523-0990

#178
Thinking Cup
Category: Coffee & Tea, Sandwiches
Average price: $11-30
Area: North End
Address: 236 Hanover St
Boston, MA 02113
Phone: (857) 233-5277

#179
Mikes City Diner
Category: Diner
Average price: Under $10
Area: South End
Address: 1714 Washington St
Boston, MA 02118
Phone: (617) 267-9393

#180
Hana Sushi
Category: Sushi Bar, Japanese
Average price: $11-30
Area: North Cambridge
Address: 2372 Massachusetts Ave
Cambridge, MA 02140
Phone: (617) 868-2121

#181
Bottega Fiorentina
Category: Italian
Average price: Under $10
Area: Coolidge Corner
Address: 313B Harvard St
Brookline, MA 02446
Phone: (617) 232-2661

#182
Darwin's Ltd
Category: Deli, Sandwiches
Average price: Under $10
Area: Harvard Square
Address: 148 Mt Auburn St
Cambridge, MA 02138
Phone: (617) 354-5233

#183
Xinh Xinh
Category: Vietnamese, Chinese
Average price: Under $10
Area: Chinatown
Address: 7 Beach St
Boston, MA 02111
Phone: (617) 422-0501

#184
Karo's BBQ
Category: Food Stands, Street Vendors
Average price: Under $10
Area: Downtown
Address: Summer & Hawley St
Boston, MA 02110
Phone: (857) 244-1174

#185
Zaftigs Delicatessen
Category: Breakfast & Brunch, Deli
Average price: $11-30
Area: Coolidge Corner
Address: 335 Harvard St
Brookline, MA 02446
Phone: (617) 975-0075

#186
Galley Diner
Category: Diner, American
Average price: Under $10
Area: South Boston
Address: 11 P St South
Boston, MA 02127
Phone: (617) 464-1024

#187
Spoke
Category: American, Wine Bar
Average price: $31-60
Area: Davis Square
Address: 89 Holland St
Somerville, MA 02144
Phone: (617) 718-9463

#188
North Street Grille
Category: Breakfast & Brunch, American
Average price: $11-30
Area: North End
Address: 229 North St
Boston, MA 02113
Phone: (617) 720-2010

#189
Theo's Cozy Corner
Category: Breakfast & Brunch, Brazilian
Average price: Under $10
Area: North End
Address: 162 Salem St
Boston, MA 02113
Phone: (617) 241-0202

#190
Ula Café
Category: Coffee & Tea, Sandwiches
Average price: Under $10
Area: Jamaica Plain
Address: 284 Amory St
Jamaica Plain, MA 02130
Phone: (617) 524-7890

#191
Bistro Du Midi
Category: French
Average price: $31-60
Area: Back Bay
Address: 272 Boylston St
Boston, MA 02116
Phone: (617) 426-7878

#192
Anchovies
Category: Italian
Average price: $11-30
Area: South End
Address: 433 Columbus Ave
Boston, MA 02116
Phone: (617) 266-5088

#193
Irashai Sushi and Teriyaki
Category: Japanese, Sushi Bar
Average price: $11-30
Area: Chinatown
Address: 8 Kneeland St
Boston, MA 02111
Phone: (617) 350-6888

#194
Yankee Lobster Fish Market
Category: Seafood Market, Seafood
Average price: $11-30
Area: Waterfront, South Boston
Address: 300 Northern Ave
Boston, MA 02210
Phone: (617) 345-9799

#195
JP Licks
Category: Ice Cream & Frozen Yogurt, Cafe
Average price: Under $10
Area: Harvard Square
Address: 1312 Massachusetts Ave
Cambridge, MA 02138
Phone: (617) 492-1001

#196
Boston Kebab House
Category: Turkish, Mediterranean
Average price: Under $10
Area: Financial District
Address: 7 Liberty Sq
Boston, MA 02109
Phone: (617) 227-6900

#197
Sip Cafe
Category: Sandwiches, Coffee & Tea
Average price: Under $10
Area: Financial District
Address: 0 Post Office Sq
Boston, MA 02109
Phone: (617) 338-3080

#198
Pomodoro
Category: Italian
Average price: $31-60
Area: Brookline Village
Address: 24 Harvard St
Brookline, MA 02445
Phone: (617) 566-4455

#199
The Boathouse
Category: American
Average price: $11-30
Area: Harvard Square
Address: 49 Mt Auburn St
Cambridge, MA 02138
Phone: (617) 349-1650

#200
Rox Diner
Category: Diner, Breakfast & Brunch
Average price: $11-30
Area: West Roxbury Center, West Roxbury
Address: 1881 Center St
West Roxbury, MA 02132
Phone: (617) 327-1909

#201
Rincon Limeño Restaurant
Category: Latin American, Peruvian
Average price: $11-30
Area: East Boston
Address: 409 Chelsea St East
Boston, MA 02128
Phone: (617) 569-4942

#202
Meritage
Category: American, Seafood
Average price: Above $61
Area: Waterfront
Address: 70 Rowes Wharf
Boston, MA 02110
Phone: (617) 439-3995

#203
Row 34
Category: American, Seafood
Average price: $31-60
Area: Waterfront, South Boston
Address: 383 Congress St
Boston, MA 02210
Phone: (617) 553-5900

#204
Limoncello Ristorante
Category: Italian, Wine Bar
Average price: $31-60
Area: North End
Address: 190 N St
Boston, MA 02127
Phone: (617) 523-4480

#205
Punjab
Category: Indian
Average price: $11-30
Area: Arlington Center
Address: 485 Massachusetts Ave
Arlington, MA 02474
Phone: (781) 643-0943

#206
Alia Ristorante
Category: Italian
Average price: $11-30
Area: Winthrop
Address: 495 Shirley St Winthrop, MA 02152
Phone: (617) 539-1600

#207
The Breakfast Club
Category: Diner, Breakfast & Brunch
Average price: Under $10
Area: Allston/Brighton
Address: 270 Western Ave
Allston, MA 02134
Phone: (617) 783-1212

#208
Yoma
Category: Burmese
Average price: $11-30
Area: Allston/Brighton
Address: 5 N Beacon St
Allston, MA 02134
Phone: (617) 783-1372

#209
Olecito
Category: Mexican
Average price: Under $10
Area: Inman Square
Address: 12 Springfield St
Cambridge, MA 02139
Phone: (617) 876-1374

#210
Stella
Category: Italian, Cafe
Average price: $31-60
Area: South End
Address: 1525 Washington St
Boston, MA 02118
Phone: (617) 247-7747

#211
SoWa Open Market
Category: Farmers Market, Food Stands
Average price: $11-30
Area: South End
Address: 460 Harrison Ave
Boston, MA 02118
Phone: (800) 403-8305

#212
The Cellar
Category: American, Bar
Average price: $11-30
Area: Central Square
Address: 991 Massachusetts Ave
Cambridge, MA 02138
Phone: (617) 876-2580

#213
Lincoln Tavern & Restaurant
Category: American, Italian
Average price: $11-30
Area: South Boston
Address: 425 W Broadway
Boston, MA 02127
Phone: (617) 765-8636

#214
Figs
Category: Pizza
Average price: $11-30
Area: Beacon Hill
Address: 42 Charles St
Boston, MA 02114
Phone: (617) 742-3447

#215
Abe & Louie's Steak House
Category: Steakhouse, Breakfast & Brunch
Average price: Above $61
Area: Back Bay
Address: 793 Boylston St
Boston, MA 02116
Phone: (617) 536-6300

#216
New England Soup Factory
Category: American, Soup
Average price: Under $10
Area: Brookline Village
Address: 2-4 Brookline Pl
Brookline, MA 02445
Phone: (617) 739-1899

#217
Sam's
Category: American, Burgers
Average price: $11-30
Area: Waterfront, South Boston
Address: 60 Northern Ave
Boston, MA 02210
Phone: (617) 295-0191

#218
La Voile
Category: French
Average price: $31-60
Area: Back Bay
Address: 261 Newbury St
Boston, MA 02116
Phone: (617) 587-4200

#219
Taiwan Café
Category: Taiwanese, Chinese
Average price: Under $10
Area: Chinatown
Address: 34 Oxford St
Boston, MA 02111
Phone: (617) 426-8181

#220
Panza
Category: Italian
Average price: $11-30
Area: North End
Address: 326 Hanover St
Boston, MA 02113
Phone: (617) 557-9248

#221
Bukowski Tavern
Category: Pub, American
Average price: $11-30
Area: Back Bay
Address: 50 Dalton St
Boston, MA 02115
Phone: (617) 437-9999

#222
Mul's Diner
Category: Diner
Average price: Under $10
Area: South Boston
Address: 75 W Broadway
Boston, MA 02127
Phone: (617) 268-5748

#223
Tatte Bakery & Cafe
Category: Bakeries, Cafe
Average price: $11-30
Area: East Cambridge, Kendall Square/MIT
Address: 318 3rd St
Mid-Cambridge, MA 02142
Phone: (617) 354-4200

#224
Piattini
Category: Italian
Average price: $11-30
Area: Back Bay
Address: 226 Newbury St
Boston, MA 02116
Phone: (617) 536-2020

#225
Grill 23 & Bar
Category: Steakhouse, Wine Bar
Average price: Above $61
Area: Back Bay
Address: 161 Berkeley St
Boston, MA 02116
Phone: (617) 542-2255

#226
Douzo
Category: Sushi Bar, Japanese
Average price: $31-60
Area: Back Bay
Address: 131 Dartmouth St
Boston, MA 02116
Phone: (617) 859-8886

#227
Mr. Dooley's
Category: Bar, Irish
Average price: $11-30
Area: Financial District
Address: 77 Broad St
Boston, MA 02109
Phone: (617) 338-5656

#228
The Paramount
Category: Breakfast & Brunch, American
Average price: $11-30
Area: Beacon Hill
Address: 44 Charles St
Boston, MA 02114
Phone: (617) 720-1152

#229
Diesel Cafe
Category: Coffee & Tea, Sandwiches
Average price: Under $10
Area: Davis Square
Address: 257 Elm St Somerville, MA 02144
Phone: (617) 629-8717

#230
Orinoco
Category: Latin American, Caribbean
Average price: $11-30
Area: Brookline Village
Address: 22 Harvard St Brookline, MA 02445
Phone: (617) 232-9505

#231
Shawarma King
Category: Middle Eastern
Average price: Under $10
Area: Coolidge Corner
Address: 1383 Beacon St Brookline, MA 02446
Phone: (617) 731-6035

#232
El Oriental De Cuba
Category: Cuban, Caribbean
Average price: $11-30
Area: Jamaica Plain
Address: 416 Centre St
Jamaica Plain, MA 02130
Phone: (617) 524-6464

#233
The Gallows
Category: American
Average price: $11-30
Area: South End
Address: 1395 Washington St
Boston, MA 02118
Phone: (617) 425-0200

#234
Sarah's Market & Cafe
Category: Grocery, Sandwiches
Average price: Under $10
Area: Huron Village
Address: 200 Concord Ave
Cambridge, MA 02138
Phone: (617) 876-5999

#235
The Similans
Category: Thai,
Average price: $11-30
Area: East Cambridge, Kendall Square/MIT
Address: 145 1st St Cambridge, MA 02142
Phone: (617) 491-6999

#236
Via Matta
Category: Italian
Average price: $31-60
Area: Back Bay
Address: 79 Park Plz
Boston, MA 02116
Phone: (617) 422-0008

#237
Shawarma Falafel
Category: Middle Eastern,
Average price: Under $10
Area: Downtown
Address: 26 Province St
Boston, MA 02108
Phone: (857) 265-3017

#238
Andala Coffee House
Category: Coffee & Tea, Middle Eastern
Average price: Under $10
Area: Central Square
Address: 286 Franklin St
Cambridge, MA 02139
Phone: (617) 945-2212

#239
Fornax Bread Company
Category: Bakeries, Soup
Average price: Under $10
Area: Roslindale Village, Roslindale
Address: 27 Corinth St Roslindale, MA 02131
Phone: (617) 325-8852

#240
Area Four
Category: Diner, Breakfast & Brunch
Average price: $11-30
Area: Kendall Square/MIT
Address: 500 Technology Sq
Cambridge, MA 02139
Phone: (617) 758-4444

#241
Falafel King
Category: Middle Eastern, Falafel
Average price: Under $10
Area: Downtown
Address: 260 Washington St
Boston, MA 02108
Phone: (617) 227-6400

#242
Twin DO-Nuts
Category: Donuts, Breakfast & Brunch
Average price: Under $10
Area: Allston/Brighton
Address: 501 Cambridge St
Allston, MA 02134
Phone: (617) 254-9421

#243
Milano's Delicatessen
Category: Deli, Pizza
Average price: Under $10
Area: East Boston
Address: 978 Saratoga St
Boston, MA 02128
Phone: (617) 567-6718

#244
Shays Pub & Wine Bar
Category: American, Wine Bar
Average price: $11-30
Area: Harvard Square
Address: 58 JFK St Cambridge, MA 02138
Phone: (617) 864-9161

#245
Bottega di Capri
Category: Specialty Food, Italian
Average price: Under $10
Area: Brookline Village
Address: 41 Harvard St
Brookline, MA 02445
Phone: (617) 738-5333

#246
Metropolis Cafe
Category: Wine Bar, Mediterranean
Average price: $11-30
Area: South End
Address: 584 Tremont St
Boston, MA 02118
Phone: (617) 247-2931

#247
Coda
Category: American, Bar
Average price: $11-30
Area: Back Bay
Address: 329 Columbus Ave
Boston, MA 02116
Phone: (617) 536-2632

#248
Rami's
Category: Middle Eastern, Kosher
Average price: $11-30
Area: Coolidge Corner
Address: 324 Harvard St
Brookline, MA 02446
Phone: (617) 738-3577

#249
Le's Restaurant
Category: Vietnamese
Average price: Under $10
Area: Allston/Brighton
Address: 137 Brighton Ave
Allston, MA 02134
Phone: (617) 783-2340

#250
Mei Sum
Category: Bakeries, Sandwiches
Average price: Under $10
Area: Chinatown
Address: 36 Beach St
Boston, MA 02111
Phone: (617) 357-4050

#251
Gyro City
Category: Greek
Average price: Under $10
Area: Fenway
Address: 88 Peterborough St
Boston, MA 02215
Phone: (617) 266-4976

#252
Boston Burger Company
Category: Burgers, Caterer
Average price: $11-30
Area: Davis Square
Address: 37 Davis Sq
Somerville, MA 02144
Phone: (617) 440-7361

#253
The Oceanaire Seafood Room
Category: Seafood
Average price: $31-60
Area: Downtown
Address: 40 Court St
Boston, MA 02108
Phone: (617) 742-2277

#254
Redd's in Rozzie
Category: American
Average price: $11-30
Area: Roslindale Village, Roslindale
Address: 4257 Washington St
Boston, MA 02131
Phone: (617) 325-1000

#255
Trattoria di Monica
Category: Italian
Average price: $31-60
Area: North End
Address: 67 Prince St
Boston, MA 02113
Phone: (617) 720-5472

#256
La Siesta
Category: Mexican
Average price: $11-30
Area: Winthrop
Address: 70-74 Woodside Ave
Winthrop, MA 02152
Phone: (617) 846-2300

#257
Rangzen Tibetan Place
Category: Food Delivery Services, Asian Fusion
Average price: $11-30
Area: Central Square
Address: 24 Pearl St
Cambridge, MA 02139
Phone: (617) 354-8881

#258
Banh Mi House
Category: Bubble Tea, Sandwiches
Average price: Under $10
Area: Downtown
Address: 48 Winter St
Boston, MA 02108
Phone: (617) 956-4039

#259
Franklin Southie
Category: American, Lounge
Average price: $11-30
Area: South Boston
Address: 152 Dorchester Ave
Boston, MA 02127
Phone: (617) 269-1003

#260
Masala
Category: Indian, Himalayan/Nepalese
Average price: $11-30
Area: Teele Square
Address: 1127 Broadway
Somerville, MA 02144
Phone: (617) 718-0703

#261
Punjabi Dhaba
Category: Indian
Average price: Under $10
Area: Inman Square
Address: 225 Hampshire St
Cambridge, MA 02139
Phone: (617) 547-8272

#262
The Beehive
Category: Jazz & Blues, American
Average price: $31-60
Area: South End
Address: 541 Tremont St
Boston, MA 02116
Phone: (617) 423-0069

#263
Espresso Love
Category: Coffee & Tea, Sandwiches
Average price: Under $10
Area: Financial District
Address: 33 Broad St
Boston, MA 02109
Phone: (857) 284-7462

#264
Caffé Vittoria
Category: Coffee & Tea, Italian
Average price: Under $10
Area: North End
Address: 296 Hanover St
Boston, MA 02113
Phone: (617) 227-7606

#265
Charlie's Sandwich Shoppe
Category: Sandwiches, Breakfast & Brunch
Average price: Under $10
Area: Back Bay
Address: 429 Columbus Ave
Boston, MA 02116
Phone: (617) 536-7669

#266
Ali's Roti Restaurant
Category: Indian, Caribbean
Average price: Under $10
Area: Mattapan
Address: 1188 Blue Hill Ave
Mattapan, MA 02126
Phone: (617) 298-9850

#267
Allston Diner
Category: Burgers, Diner
Average price: $11-30
Area: Allston/Brighton
Address: 431 Cambridge St
Allston, MA 02134
Phone: (617) 208-8741

#268
New Dong Khanh
Category: Vietnamese, Chinese
Average price: Under $10
Area: Chinatown
Address: 81 Harrison Ave
Boston, MA 02111
Phone: (617) 426-9410

#269
Winsor Dim Sum Café
Category: Dim Sum
Average price: Under $10
Area: Chinatown
Address: 10 Tyler St
Boston, MA 02111
Phone: (617) 338-1688

#270
Dino's Cafe
Category: Italian, Deli
Average price: Under $10
Area: North End
Address: 141 Salem St
Boston, MA 02113
Phone: (617) 227-1991

#271
Ecco Pizzeria
Category: Pizza, Salad
Average price: $11-30
Area: Allston/Brighton
Address: 1147 Commonwealth Ave
Boston, MA 02134
Phone: (617) 903-4324

#272
Sweetgreen
Category: Salad, Gluten-Free
Average price: $11-30
Area: Back Bay
Address: 659 Boylston St
Boston, MA 02116
Phone: (617) 936-3464

#273
Puritan & Company
Category: American, Cocktail Bar
Average price: $31-60
Area: Inman Square
Address: 1166 Cambridge St
Cambridge, MA 02139
Phone: (617) 615-6195

#274
Clio Restaurant
Category: American, Seafood
Average price: Above $61
Area: Back Bay
Address: 370 Commonwealth Ave
Boston, MA 02215
Phone: (617) 536-7200

#275
New Saigon Sandwich
Category: Deli, Vietnamese
Average price: Under $10
Area: Chinatown
Address: 696 Washington St
Boston, MA 02111
Phone: (617) 542-6296

#276
J J Foley's Cafe
Category: Pub, American
Average price: $11-30
Area: South End
Address: 117 E Berkeley St
Boston, MA 02118
Phone: (617) 728-9101

#277
The Squealing Pig
Category: Pub, Breakfast & Brunch
Average price: $11-30
Area: Mission Hill
Address: 134 Smith St Roxbury
Crossing, MA 02120
Phone: (617) 566-6651

#278
Cafe Kiraz
Category: Sandwiches, Deli
Average price: Under $10
Area: Inman Square
Address: 119 Hampshire St
Cambridge, MA 02139
Phone: (617) 868-2233

#279
Scullers Jazz Club
Category: Jazz & Blues, American
Average price: $11-30
Area: Allston/Brighton
Address: 400 Soldiers Rd
Boston, MA 02134
Phone: (617) 562-4111

#280
75 Chestnut
Category: American, Diner
Average price: $11-30
Area: Beacon Hill
Address: 75 Chestnut St
Boston, MA 02108
Phone: (617) 227-2175

#281
The Blue Room
Category: Mediterranean
Average price: $31-60
Area: Kendall Square/MIT
Address: 1 Kendall Sq,
Ste 200 Cambridge, MA 02139
Phone: (617) 494-9034

#282
Brookline Lunch
Category: Diner, Middle Eastern
Average price: Under $10
Area: Central Square
Address: 9 Brookline St
Cambridge, MA 02138
Phone: (617) 354-2983

#283
City Bar
Category: Lounge, American
Average price: $31-60
Area: Back Bay
Address: 61 Exeter St
Boston, MA 02199
Phone: (617) 536-5300

#284
La Famiglia Giorgio's
Category: Italian, Gluten-Free
Average price: $11-30
Area: North End
Address: 112 Salem St
Boston, MA 02113
Phone: (617) 367-6711

#285
Fiore's Bakery
Category: Bakeries, Vegan
Average price: Under $10
Area: Jamaica Plain
Address: 55 South St
Jamaica Plain, MA 02130
Phone: (617) 524-9200

#286
Thai Moon
Category: Thai
Average price: $11-30
Area: Arlington Center
Address: 663 Massachusetts Ave
Arlington, MA 02476
Phone: (781) 646-3334

#287
Soul Fire BBQ
Category: Barbeque
Average price: $11-30
Area: Allston/Brighton
Address: 182 Harvard Ave
Allston, MA 02134
Phone: (617) 787-3003

#288
L'Impasto
Category: Italian
Average price: $11-30
Area: North Cambridge
Address: 2263 Massachusetts Ave
Cambridge, MA 02140
Phone: (617) 491-1901

#289
Village Sushi & Grill
Category: Sushi Bar, Japanese
Average price: $11-30
Area: Roslindale Village, Roslindale
Address: 14 Corinth St Roslindale, MA 02131
Phone: (617) 363-7874

#290
McKenna's Cafe
Category: American, Breakfast & Brunch
Average price: Under $10
Area: Dorchester
Address: 109 Savin Hill Ave
Dorchester, MA 02125
Phone: (617) 825-8218

#291
Scollay Square
Category: Seafood, American
Average price: $11-30
Area: Downtown, Beacon Hill
Address: 21 Beacon St
Boston, MA 02108
Phone: (617) 742-4900

#292
Paris Creperie
Category: Creperies, Caterer
Average price: Under $10
Area: Coolidge Corner
Address: 278 Harvard St
Brookline, MA 02446
Phone: (617) 232-1770

#293
Bon Chon
Category: Korean, Japanese
Average price: $11-30
Area: Allston/Brighton
Address: 123 Brighton Ave
Allston, MA 02134
Phone: (617) 254-8888

#294
The Banshee
Category: Pub, Irish
Average price: $11-30
Area: Dorchester
Address: 934 Dorchester Ave
Dorchester, MA 02125
Phone: (617) 436-9747

#295
Cafe Barada
Category: Caterer, Middle Eastern
Average price: $11-30
Area: North Cambridge
Address: 2269 Massachusetts Ave
Cambridge, MA 02140
Phone: (617) 354-4446

#296
Rod Dee Thai Cuisine
Category: Thai
Average price: Under $10
Area: Porter Square
Address: 1906 Massachusetts Ave
Cambridge, MA 02140
Phone: (617) 374-9252

#297
The Regal Beagle
Category: Bar, American
Average price: $11-30
Area: Coolidge Corner
Address: 308 Harvard St
Brookline, MA 02446
Phone: (617) 739-5151

#298
MJ Ready International Bistro
Category: Thai, Italian
Average price: Under $10
Area: Coolidge Corner
Address: 318 Harvard St
Brookline, MA 02446
Phone: (857) 576-4225

#299
Azama Grill
Category: Middle Eastern, Halal
Average price: Under $10
Area: Allston/Brighton
Address: 54 Harvard Ave
Allston, MA 02134
Phone: (617) 779-0003

#300
Boloco
Category: American
Average price: Under $10
Area: Financial District
Address: 133 Federal St
Boston, MA 02110
Phone: (617) 357-9727

Boston Restaurant Guide / Restaurants, Bars & Cafés

#301
Cafe Sushi
Category: Sushi Bar, Japanese
Average price: $11-30
Area: Harvard Square
Address: 1105 Massachusetts Ave
Cambridge, MA 02138
Phone: (617) 492-0434

#302
Wai Wai Restaurant
Category: Chinese
Average price: Under $10
Area: Chinatown
Address: 26 Oxford St
Boston, MA 02111
Phone: (617) 338-9833

#303
Newtowne Variety
Category: Sandwiches, Salad
Average price: Under $10
Area: Kendall Square/MIT
Address: 93 Windsor St
Cambridge, MA 02139
Phone: (617) 868-5112

#304
Izzy's Restaurant & Sub Shop
Category: American, Sandwiches
Average price: Under $10
Area: Kendall Square/MIT
Address: 169 Harvard St
Cambridge, MA 02139
Phone: (617) 661-3910

#305
Paraiso Restaurant
Category: Spanish
Average price: $11-30
Area: Dorchester, Uphams Corner
Address: 750 Dudley St
Boston, MA 02125
Phone: (617) 265-7067

#306
Tenoch Mexican
Category: Mexican
Average price: Under $10
Area: North End
Address: 3 Lewis St
Boston, MA 02110
Phone: (617) 248-9537

#307
Jac's Cafe
Category: Breakfast & Brunch
Average price: Under $10
Area: Winthrop
Address: 29 Crest Ave
Winthrop, MA 02152
Phone: (617) 846-7496

#308
Figs
Category: Pizza, Italian
Average price: $11-30
Area: Charlestown
Address: 67 Main St
Charlestown, MA 02129
Phone: (617) 242-2229

#309
Cambridge, 1.
Category: Pizza
Average price: $11-30
Area: Harvard Square
Address: 27 Church St Cambridge, MA 02138
Phone: (617) 576-1111

#310
Mirisola's
Category: Italian, Pizza
Average price: Under $10
Area: South Boston
Address: 200 L St
Boston, MA 02127
Phone: (617) 269-9701

#311
Tasty Burger
Category: Burgers, Hot Dogs
Average price: Under $10
Area: Fenway
Address: 1301-05 Boylston St
Boston, MA 02215
Phone: (617) 425-4444

#312
Saigon Hut
Category: Vietnamese
Average price: Under $10
Area: East Boston
Address: 305 Meridian St East
Boston, MA 02128
Phone: (617) 567-1944

#313
Mela
Category: Indian
Average price: $11-30
Area: South End
Address: 578 Tremont St
Boston, MA 02118
Phone: (617) 859-4805

#314
Cambridge Common
Category: American, Bar
Average price: $11-30
Area: Porter Square
Address: 1667 Massachusetts Ave
Cambridge, MA 02138
Phone: (617) 547-1228

#315
Citizen Public House & Oyster Bar
Category: GastroPub
Average price: $31-60
Area: Fenway
Address: 1310 Boylston St
Boston, MA 02215
Phone: (617) 450-9000

#316
Sophia's Grotto
Category: Italian, Spanish
Average price: $11-30
Area: Roslindale Village, Roslindale
Address: 22 Birch St
Roslindale, MA 02131
Phone: (617) 323-4595

#317
Anna's Taqueria
Category: Mexican
Average price: Under $10
Area: Davis Square
Address: 236 Elm St
Somerville, MA 02144
Phone: (617) 666-3900

#318
Mehak
Category: Indian, Pakistani
Average price: $11-30
Area: East Boston
Address: 329 Sumner St
Boston, MA 02128
Phone: (617) 567-1900

#319
West Side Lounge
Category: Lounge, American
Average price: $11-30
Area: Porter Square
Address: 1680 Massachusetts Ave
Cambridge, MA 02138
Phone: (617) 441-5566

#320
Lucky's Lounge
Category: Lounge, American
Average price: $11-30
Area: Waterfront, South Boston
Address: 355 Congress St
Boston, MA 02210
Phone: (617) 357-5825

#321
Centre Street Café
Category: Breakfast & Brunch, American
Average price: $11-30
Area: Jamaica Plain
Address: 669A Centre St
Boston, MA 02130
Phone: (617) 524-9217

#322
Angelo's Pizza
Category: Pizza
Average price: Under $10
Area: Harvard Square
Address: 444 Broadway
Cambridge, MA 02138
Phone: (617) 661-8049

#323
Matt Murphy's Pub
Category: Pub, Irish
Average price: $11-30
Area: Brookline Village
Address: 14 Harvard St
Brookline, MA 02445
Phone: (617) 232-0188

#324
Baraka Café
Category: African, Mediterranean
Average price: $11-30
Area: Central Square
Address: 80 Pearl St
Cambridge, MA 02139
Phone: (617) 868-3951

#325
Sakanaya
Category: Seafood, Japanese
Average price: $11-30
Area: Allston/Brighton
Address: 75 Linden St
Boston, MA 02134
Phone: (617) 254-0009

#326
Los Amigos
Category: Tex-Mex, Mexican
Average price: Under $10
Area: West Roxbury Center, West Roxbury
Address: 1743 Centre St
West Roxbury, MA 02132
Phone: (617) 477-4472

#327
Temple Bar
Category: American, Bar
Average price: $11-30
Area: Porter Square
Address: 1688 Massachusetts Ave
Cambridge, MA 02138
Phone: (617) 547-5055

#328
Davio's
Category: Italian, Steakhouse
Average price: $31-60
Area: Back Bay
Address: 75 Arlington St
Boston, MA 02116
Phone: (617) 357-4810

#329
dbar
Category: Dance Clubs, American
Average price: $11-30
Area: Dorchester
Address: 1236 Dorchester Ave
Dorchester, MA 02125
Phone: (617) 265-4490

#330
May's Fusion and Cuisine
Category: Taiwanese
Average price: $11-30
Area: Allston/Brighton
Address: 95 Glenville Ave
Allston, MA 02134
Phone: (617) 782-1688

#331
Q Restaurant
Category: Chinese, Sushi Bar
Average price: $11-30
Area: Chinatown
Address: 660 Washington St
Boston, MA 02111
Phone: (857) 350-3968

#332
Olga's Kafe
Category: Breakfast & Brunch, Coffee & Tea
Average price: Under $10
Area: Financial District
Address: 99 Summer St
Boston, MA 02110
Phone: (617) 204-9808

#333
Gourmet Dumpling House
Category: Chinese, Taiwanese
Average price: $11-30
Area: Chinatown
Address: 52 Beach St
Boston, MA 02111
Phone: (617) 338-6223

#334
Trident Booksellers & Café
Category: Bookstores, Breakfast & Brunch
Average price: $11-30
Area: Back Bay
Address: 338 Newbury St
Boston, MA 02115
Phone: (617) 267-8688

#335
OggiGourmet
Category: Pizza, Sandwiches
Average price: Under $10
Area: Harvard Square
Address: 1350 Massachusetts Ave
Cambridge, MA 02138
Phone: (617) 830-6657

#336
Olé Mexican Grill
Category: Mexican
Average price: $31-60
Area: Inman Square
Address: 11 Springfield St
Cambridge, MA 02139
Phone: (617) 492-4495

#337
Central Kitchen
Category: American
Average price: $31-60
Area: Central Square
Address: 567 Massachusetts Ave
Cambridge, MA 02139
Phone: (617) 491-5599

#338
Sushi Station
Category: Japanese, Sushi Bar
Average price: $11-30
Area: Mission Hill
Address: 1562 Tremont St
Boston, MA 02120
Phone: (617) 738-0888

#339
Border Café
Category: Tex-Mex, Cajun/Creole
Average price: $11-30
Area: Harvard Square
Address: 32 Church St
Cambridge, MA 02138
Phone: (617) 864-6100

#340
Kitchen
Category: American, American
Average price: $31-60
Area: South End
Address: 560 Tremont St
Boston, MA 02118
Phone: (617) 695-1250

#341
The Courtyard Restaurant
Category: American
Average price: $11-30
Area: Back Bay
Address: 230 Darmouth St
Boston, MA 02116
Phone: (617) 859-2282

#342
Pedro's Tacos
Category: Mexican
Average price: Under $10
Area: Downtown
Address: 55 Bromfield St
Boston, MA 02108
Phone: (617) 482-8822

#343
Corner Cafe
Category: Dive Bar, American
Average price: Under $10
Area: North End
Address: 87 Prince St
Boston, MA 02113
Phone: (617) 523-8997

#344
Himalayan Bistro
Category: Himalayan/Nepalese, Indian
Average price: $11-30
Area: West Roxbury Center, West Roxbury
Address: 1735 Center St
West Roxbury, MA 02132
Phone: (617) 325-3500

#345
Henrietta's Table
Category: American, Desserts
Average price: $31-60
Area: Harvard Square
Address: 1 Bennett St
Cambridge, MA 02138
Phone: (617) 661-5005

#346
Evoo Restaurant
Category: American
Average price: $31-60
Area: East Cambridge, Kendall Square/MIT
Address: 350 3rd St Cambridge, MA 02142
Phone: (617) 661-3866

#347
Viga Eatery & Catering
Category: Italian, Sandwiches
Average price: Under $10
Area: Financial District
Address: 133 Pearl St
Boston, MA 02110
Phone: (617) 482-1112

#348
Banh Mi Ba Le
Category: Vietnamese, Sandwiches
Average price: Under $10
Area: Dorchester
Address: 1052 Dorchester Ave
Dorchester, MA 02125
Phone: (617) 265-7171

#349
Les Zygomates
Category: French, Jazz & Blues
Average price: $31-60
Area: Waterfront, Leather District, South Boston
Address: 129 South St
Boston, MA 02111
Phone: (617) 542-5108

#350
My Thai Vegan Cafe
Category: Thai, Vegan
Average price: $11-30
Area: Chinatown
Address: 3 Beach St
Boston, MA 02111
Phone: (617) 451-2395

#351
Teranga
Category: Bar, Senegalese
Average price: $11-30
Area: South End
Address: 1746 Washington St
Boston, MA 02118
Phone: (617) 266-0003

#352
Legal Harborside
Category: Seafood, American
Average price: $31-60
Area: Waterfront, South Boston
Address: 270 Northern Ave
Boston, MA 02210
Phone: (617) 477-2900

#353
Johnny D's
Category: Bar, Breakfast & Brunch
Average price: $11-30
Area: Davis Square
Address: 17 Holland St
Somerville, MA 02144
Phone: (617) 776-2004

#354
Hong Kong Eatery
Category: Cantonese
Average price: Under $10
Area: Chinatown
Address: 79 Harrison Ave
Boston, MA 02111
Phone: (617) 423-0838

#355
Redbones
Category: Barbeque, Bar
Average price: $11-30
Area: Davis Square
Address: 55 Chester St Somerville, MA 02144
Phone: (617) 628-2200

#356
Tango Restaurant
Category: Latin American, Steakhouse
Average price: $31-60
Area: Arlington Center
Address: 464 Massachusetts Ave
Arlington, MA 02474
Phone: (781) 443-9000

#357
Grasshopper Restaurant
Category: Chinese, Vietnamese
Average price: $11-30
Area: Allston/Brighton
Address: 1 N Beacon St
Allston, MA 02134
Phone: (617) 254-8883

#358
Cafe Fleuri
Category: French, Cafe
Average price: $31-60
Area: Financial District
Address: 250 Franklin St
Boston, MA 02110
Phone: (617) 451-1900

#359
JP Seafood Cafe
Category: Japanese, Korean
Average price: $11-30
Area: Jamaica Plain
Address: 730 Ctr St
Jamaica Plain, MA 02130
Phone: (617) 983-5177

#360
Tremont 647
Category: Bar, American
Average price: $11-30
Area: South End
Address: 647 Tremont St
Boston, MA 02118
Phone: (617) 266-4600

#361
Legal Sea Foods
Category: Seafood
Average price: $11-30
Area: East Boston
Address: 1 Harborside Dr
Boston, MA 02128
Phone: (617) 568-2811

#362
Shabu-Zen
Category: Japanese
Average price: $11-30
Area: Allston/Brighton
Address: 80 Brighton Ave
Allston, MA 02134
Phone: (617) 782-8888

#363
Mooo....
Category: Steakhouse
Average price: Above $61
Area: Downtown
Address: 15 Beacon St
Boston, MA 02108
Phone: (617) 670-2515

#364
Jo Jo TaiPei
Category: Taiwanese, Chinese
Average price: $11-30
Area: Allston/Brighton
Address: 103 Brighton Ave
Allston, MA 02134
Phone: (617) 254-8889

#365
My Cousin's Place
Category: Cafe, Coffee & Tea
Average price: Under $10
Area: North End
Address: 396 Hanover St
Boston, MA 02113
Phone: (857) 350-3029

#366
Vee Vee
Category: American
Average price: $11-30
Area: Jamaica Plain
Address: 763 Centre St
Jamaica Plain, MA 02130
Phone: (617) 522-0145

#367
Liberty Bell Roast Beef
Category: Sandwiches, Pizza
Average price: Under $10
Area: South Boston
Address: 170 W Broadway
Boston, MA 02127
Phone: (617) 269-3909

#368
Little Q Hot Pot
Category: Chinese
Average price: $11-30
Area: East Arlington
Address: 196 Massachusetts Ave
Arlington, MA 02474
Phone: (781) 488-3755

#369
Terramia Ristorante
Category: Italian
Average price: $31-60
Area: North End
Address: 98 Salem St
Boston, MA 02113
Phone: (617) 523-3112

#370
Shanghai Gate
Category: Chinese
Average price: $11-30
Area: Allston/Brighton
Address: 204 Harvard Ave
Allston, MA 02134
Phone: (617) 566-7344

#371
Masa
Category: American, Mexican
Average price: $11-30
Area: South End
Address: 439 Tremont St
Boston, MA 02116
Phone: (617) 338-8884

#372
Felipe's Taqueria
Category: Mexican
Average price: Under $10
Area: Harvard Square
Address: 83 Mt Auburn St
Cambridge, MA 02138
Phone: (617) 354-9944

#373
Lolita Cocina & Tequila Bar
Category: Mexican, Lounge
Average price: $31-60
Area: Back Bay
Address: 271 Dartmouth St
Boston, MA 02116
Phone: (617) 369-5609

#374
Carmelina's
Category: Italian
Average price: $31-60
Area: North End
Address: 307 Hanover St
Boston, MA 02113
Phone: (617) 742-0020

#375
Antico Forno
Category: Italian
Average price: $11-30
Area: North End
Address: 93 Salem St
Boston, MA 02113
Phone: (617) 723-6733

#376
Alfredo's Italian Kitchen
Category: Italian, Pizza
Average price: Under $10
Area: South Boston
Address: 243 Dorchester St South
Boston, MA 02127
Phone: (617) 268-8939

#377
Pikaichi
Category: Japanese
Average price: Under $10
Area: Allston/Brighton
Address: 1 Brighton Ave
Boston, MA 02134
Phone: (617) 789-4818

#378
Toscano
Category: Italian
Average price: $11-30
Area: Harvard Square
Address: 52 Brattle St
Cambridge, MA 02138
Phone: (617) 354-5250

#379
Local 149
Category: Pub, American
Average price: $11-30
Area: South Boston
Address: 149 P St
Boston, MA 02127
Phone: (617) 269-0900

#380
The Field
Category: Pub, Burgers
Average price: Under $10
Area: Central Square
Address: 20 Prospect St
Cambridge, MA 02139
Phone: (617) 354-7345

#381
Baltic Deli & Cafe
Category: Deli, Ethnic Food
Average price: Under $10
Area: South Boston
Address: 632 Dorchester Ave
Boston, MA 02127
Phone: (617) 268-2435

#382
Sabur
Category: Mediterranean
Average price: $31-60
Area: Teele Square
Address: 212 Holland St
Somerville, MA 02144
Phone: (617) 776-7890

#383
Fill-A-Buster
Category: Deli, Salad
Average price: Under $10
Area: Downtown, Beacon Hill
Address: 142 Bowdoin St
Boston, MA 02108
Phone: (617) 523-8164

#384
Alex's Chimis
Category: Caribbean
Average price: Under $10
Area: Jamaica Plain
Address: 358 Centre St
Jamaica Plain, MA 02130
Phone: (617) 522-5201

#385
Sweet Touch Cafe
Category: Coffee & Tea, Sandwiches
Average price: Under $10
Area: East Cambridge
Address: 241 Cambridge St
Cambridge, MA 02141
Phone: (617) 491-4119

#386
Harry's Bar & Grill
Category: Bar, American
Average price: $11-30
Area: Allston/Brighton
Address: 1430 Commonwealth Ave
Brighton, MA 02135
Phone: (617) 738-9990

#387
Spike's Junkyard Dogs
Category: Hot Dogs
Average price: Under $10
Area: Allston/Brighton
Address: 108 Brighton Ave
Allston, MA 02134
Phone: (617) 254-7700

#388
Back Bay Sandwich
Category: Sandwiches
Average price: Under $10
Area: Back Bay
Address: 31 St James Ave
Boston, MA 02116
Phone: (617) 451-1561

#389
Tangierino
Category: Moroccan, African
Average price: $31-60
Area: Charlestown
Address: 83 Main St
Charlestown, MA 02129
Phone: (617) 242-6009

#390
Carmen Trattoria
Category: Italian
Average price: $31-60
Area: North End
Address: 33 North Sq
Boston, MA 02113
Phone: (617) 742-6421

#391
Addis Red Sea
Category: Ethiopian
Average price: $11-30
Area: South End
Address: 544 Tremont St
Boston, MA 02116
Phone: (617) 426-8727

#392
La Summa
Category: Italian
Average price: $11-30
Area: North End
Address: 30 Fleet St
Boston, MA 02113
Phone: (617) 523-9503

#393
Neighborhoods Coffee & Crepes
Category: Coffee & Tea, Cafe
Average price: Under $10
Area: Fenway
Address: 96 Peterborough St
Boston, MA 02215
Phone: (617) 262-7700

#394
Dough East Boston
Category: Pizza, Sandwiches
Average price: Under $10
Area: East Boston
Address: 20 Maverick St East
Boston, MA 02128
Phone: (617) 567-8787

#395
Viga Italian Eatery & Caterer
Category: Italian
Average price: Under $10
Area: Downtown
Address: 291 Devonshire St
Boston, MA 02110
Phone: (617) 482-1113

#396
Qing Dao Garden
Category: Chinese, Seafood
Average price: $11-30
Area: North Cambridge
Address: 2382 Massachusetts Ave
Cambridge, MA 02138
Phone: (617) 492-7540

#397
Berkeley Perk Cafe
Category: Sandwiches, Coffee & Tea
Average price: Under $10
Area: South End
Address: 69 Berkeley St
Boston, MA 02116
Phone: (617) 426-7375

#398
Harvest of India
Category: Indian, Pakistani
Average price: $11-30
Area: Central Square
Address: 1001 Massachusetts Ave
Cambridge, MA 02138
Phone: (617) 441-4034

#399
Myung Dong 1st Ave
Category: Korean, Bar
Average price: $11-30
Area: Allston/Brighton
Address: 90-92 Harvard Ave
Allston, MA 02134
Phone: (617) 206-3229

#400
Dado Tea
Category: Coffee & Tea, Sandwiches
Average price: Under $10
Area: Central Square
Address: 955 Massachusetts Ave
Cambridge, MA 02139
Phone: (617) 497-9061

#401
Cactus Mexican Grill
Category: Mexican
Average price: Under $10
Area: East Boston
Address: 44 Maverick Sq
Boston, MA 02128
Phone: (617) 561-2800

#402
Stoddard's Fine Food & Ale
Category: Bar, American
Average price: $11-30
Area: Downtown
Address: 48 Temple Pl
Boston, MA 02111
Phone: (617) 426-0048

#403
The Pour House
Category: Bar, American
Average price: Under $10
Area: Back Bay
Address: 907 Boylston St
Boston, MA 02115
Phone: (617) 236-1767

#404
Grass Roots Cafe
Category: Sandwiches, Korean
Average price: Under $10
Area: Downtown
Address: 101 Arch St
Boston, MA 02110
Phone: (617) 951-2124

#405
The Goods JP
Category: American
Average price: Under $10
Area: Jamaica Plain
Address: 378 Centre St
Boston, MA 02130
Phone: (617) 522-1210

#406
Estragon
Category: Tapas Bar, Spanish
Average price: $11-30
Area: South End
Address: 700 Harrison Ave
Boston, MA 02118
Phone: (617) 266-0443

#407
Five Horses Tavern
Category: American, Pub
Average price: $11-30
Area: Davis Square
Address: 400 Highland Ave
Somerville, MA 02144
Phone: (617) 764-1655

#408
Knight Moves
Category: Cafe
Average price: Under $10
Area: Coolidge Corner
Address: 1402 Beacon St
Brookline, MA 02446
Phone: (617) 487-5259

#409
ZuZu
Category: Mediterranean, Italian
Average price: $11-30
Area: Central Square
Address: 474 Massachusetts Ave
Cambridge, MA 02139
Phone: (617) 864-3278

#410
Regina Pizzeria
Category: Pizza, Italian
Average price: $11-30
Area: Allston/Brighton
Address: 353 Cambridge Street
Allston, MA 02134
Phone: (617) 783-2300

#411
Ostra
Category: Seafood, Mediterranean
Average price: Above $61
Area: Back Bay
Address: 1 Charles St S
Boston, MA 02116
Phone: (617) 421-1200

#412
Cambridge Deli & Grill
Category: Deli, American
Average price: Under $10
Area: Central Square
Address: 90 River St
Cambridge, MA 02139
Phone: (617) 868-6740

#413
The Goods JP
Category: American
Average price: Under $10
Area: Jamaica Plain
Address: 378 Centre St
Boston, MA 02130
Phone: (617) 522-1210

#414
163 Vietnamese Sandwiches & Bubble Tea
Category: Vietnamese, Coffee & Tea
Average price: Under $10
Area: Chinatown
Address: 66 Harrison Ave
Boston, MA 02111
Phone: (617) 542-7903

#415
Nico Ristorante
Category: Italian
Average price: $31-60
Area: North End
Address: 417 Hanover St
Boston, MA 02113
Phone: (617) 742-0404

#416
Rialto
Category: Italian
Average price: $31-60
Area: Harvard Square
Address: 1 Bennett St
Cambridge, MA 02138
Phone: (617) 661-5050

#417
Cafe Mamtaz
Category: Indian
Average price: $11-30
Area: South Boston
Address: 87 L St
Boston, MA 02127
Phone: (617) 464-4800

#418
Tip Tap Room
Category: American, Bar
Average price: $11-30
Area: Beacon Hill
Address: 138 Cambridge St
Boston, MA 02114
Phone: (857) 350-3344

#419
Lucca
Category: Italian
Average price: $31-60
Area: North End
Address: 226 Hanover St
Boston, MA 02113
Phone: (617) 742-9200

#420
Christopher's
Category: Bar, American
Average price: $11-30
Area: Porter Square
Address: 1920 Massachusetts Ave
Cambridge, MA 02140
Phone: (617) 876-9180

#421
Hidyan Café
Category: Ice Cream,
Frozen Yogurt, American
Average price: Under $10
Area: Fenway
Address: 80 Kilmarnock St
Boston, MA 02215
Phone: (617) 437-0966

#422
Aceituna Cafe
Category: Middle Eastern
Average price: Under $10
Area: East Cambridge, Kendall Square/MIT
Address: 605 W Kendall St
Cambridge, MA 02142
Phone: (617) 252-0707

#423
Peach Farm
Category: Chinese
Average price: $11-30
Area: Chinatown
Address: 4 Tyler St
Boston, MA 02111
Phone: (617) 482-1116

#424
Sabatino's Italian Kitchen
Category: Italian, Pizza
Average price: Under $10
Area: East Arlington
Address: 242 Massachusetts Ave
Arlington, MA 02476
Phone: (781) 646-4126

#425
Strega Waterfront
Category: Italian
Average price: $31-60
Area: Waterfront, South Boston
Address: One Marina Park Dr
Boston, MA 02210
Phone: (617) 345-3992

#426
Viga
Category: Italian
Average price: Under $10
Area: Back Bay
Address: 304 Stuart St
Boston, MA 02116
Phone: (617) 542-7200

#427
City Landing
Category: American
Average price: $31-60
Area: Waterfront
Address: 255 State St
Boston, MA 02109
Phone: (617) 725-0305

#428
Frio Rico
Category: Latin American, Grocery
Average price: Under $10
Area: East Boston
Address: 360 R Bennington St East
Boston, MA 02128
Phone: (617) 569-1505

#429
Mare
Category: Italian, Seafood
Average price: $31-60
Area: North End
Address: 135 Richmond St
Boston, MA 02109
Phone: (617) 723-6273

#430
Boston Kabob Company
Category: Middle Eastern, Halal
Average price: Under $10
Area: Allston/Brighton
Address: 164 Brighton Ave
Allston, MA 02134
Phone: (617) 254-2333

#431
Tavern at the End of the World
Category: Pub, American
Average price: $11-30
Area: Charlestown
Address: 108 Cambridge St
Charlestown, MA 02129
Phone: (617) 241-4999

#432
Stephi's on Tremont
Category: American
Average price: $11-30
Area: South End
Address: 571 Tremont St
Boston, MA 02118
Phone: (617) 236-2063

#433
James Gate
Category: Pub, American
Average price: $11-30
Area: Jamaica Plain
Address: 5 McBride St
Jamaica Plain, MA 02130
Phone: (617) 983-2000

#434
Casa Romero
Category: Mexican
Average price: $11-30
Area: Back Bay
Address: 30 Gloucester St
Boston, MA 02115
Phone: (617) 536-4341

#435
Thelonious Monkfish
Category: Sushi Bar, Japanese
Average price: $11-30
Area: Central Square
Address: 524 Massachusetts Ave
Cambridge, MA 02139
Phone: (617) 441-2116

#436
Saraceno
Category: Italian
Average price: $11-30
Area: North End
Address: 286 Hanover St
Boston, MA 02113
Phone: (617) 227-5353

#437
Maurizios
Category: Italian
Average price: $11-30
Area: North End
Address: 364 Hanover St
Boston, MA 02113
Phone: (617) 367-1123

#438
New Jumbo Seafood Restaurant
Category: Seafood, Chinese
Average price: $11-30
Area: Chinatown
Address: 5-9 Hudson St
Boston, MA 02111
Phone: (617) 542-2823

#439
Battery Park Bar & Lounge
Category: American, Lounge
Average price: $11-30
Area: Financial District
Address: 33 Batterymarch St
Boston, MA 02110
Phone: (617) 350-7275

#440
Cafe Beirut
Category: Lebanese
Average price: Under $10
Area: Jamaica Plain
Address: 654 Centre St
Jamaica Plain, MA 02130
Phone: (617) 522-7264

#441
Legal Sea Foods
Category: Seafood
Average price: $31-60
Area: Waterfront
Address: 255 State St
Boston, MA 02109
Phone: (617) 742-5300

#442
Pat's Pizza
Category: Pizza
Average price: Under $10
Area: Dorchester
Address: 2254 Dorchester Ave
Dorchester Center, MA 02124
Phone: (617) 298-9625

#443
Buccieri's Cafe
Category: Italian, Deli
Average price: Under $10
Area: Financial District
Address: 260 Franklin St
Boston, MA 02110
Phone: (617) 330-5355

#444
MuLan
Category: Taiwanese
Average price: $11-30
Area: Kendall Square/MIT
Address: 228 Broadway
Cambridge, MA 02139
Phone: (617) 441-8812

#445
Violette Gluten Free Bakery
Category: Bakeries, Coffee & Tea
Average price: $11-30
Area: Central Square
Address: 1001 Massachusetts Ave
Cambridge, MA 02139
Phone: (617) 945-7660

#446
OTTO
Category: Pizza
Average price: $11-30
Area: Coolidge Corner
Address: 289 Harvard St
Brookline, MA 02446
Phone: (617) 232-0014

#447
Del Frisco's Double Eagle Steak House
Category: Seafood, Steakhouse
Average price: Above $61
Area: Waterfront, South Boston
Address: 250 Northern Ave
Boston, MA 02210
Phone: (617) 951-1368

#448
Singh's Roti Shop
Category: Caribbean
Average price: Under $10
Area: Dorchester
Address: 692 Columbia Rd
Dorchester, MA 02125
Phone: (617) 282-7977

#449
Royal Roast Beef & Seafood
Category: Seafood, American
Average price: Under $10
Area: East Boston
Address: 752 Bennington St
Boston, MA 02128
Phone: (617) 567-7779

#450
Que Padre
Category: Mexican
Average price: Under $10
Area: East Boston
Address: 386 Chelsea St
Boston, MA 02128
Phone: (617) 418-7278

#451
Maggiano's Little Italy
Category: Italian
Average price: $11-30
Area: Back Bay
Address: 4 Columbus Ave
Boston, MA 02116
Phone: (617) 542-3456

#452
Ward 8
Category: Cocktail Bar, American
Average price: $11-30
Area: North End
Address: 90 N Washington St
Boston, MA 02113
Phone: (617) 823-4478

#453
El Paisa Orient Heights
Category: Colombian
Average price: $11-30
Area: East Boston
Address: 1012 Bennington St
Boston, MA 02128
Phone: (617) 569-5267

#454
The Warren Tavern
Category: Bar, American
Average price: $11-30
Area: Charlestown
Address: 2 Pleasant St
Charlestown, MA 02129
Phone: (617) 241-8142

#455
Bon Chon
Category: Korean, Barbeque
Average price: $11-30
Area: Harvard Square
Address: 57 John F Kennedy St
Cambridge, MA 02138
Phone: (617) 868-0981

#456
Phu-ket Thai
Category: Thai
Average price: $11-30
Area: West Roxbury Center, West Roxbury
Address: 1856 Centre St
West Roxbury, MA 02132
Phone: (617) 469-5200

#457
Mr. Bartley's Gourmet Burgers
Category: Burgers
Average price: $11-30
Area: Harvard Square
Address: 1246 Massachusetts Ave
Cambridge, MA 02138
Phone: (617) 354-6559

#458
The Maharaja
Category: Indian
Average price: $11-30
Area: Harvard Square
Address: 57 JFK St
Cambridge, MA 02138
Phone: (617) 547-2757

#459
Rendezvous In Central Square
Category: American
Average price: $31-60
Area: Central Square
Address: 502 Massachusetts Ave
Cambridge, MA 02139
Phone: (617) 576-1900

#460
Thaitation
Category: Thai
Average price: $11-30
Area: Fenway
Address: 129 Jersey St
Boston, MA 02215
Phone: (617) 585-9909

#461
Café Jaffa
Category: Middle Eastern
Average price: $11-30
Area: Back Bay
Address: 48 Gloucester St
Boston, MA 02115
Phone: (617) 536-0230

#462
Bravo Pizza
Category: Pizza, Ice Cream & Frozen Yogurt
Average price: Under $10
Area: Allston/Brighton
Address: 160 Brighton Ave
Allston, MA 02134
Phone: (617) 782-0882

#463
Yokohama
Category: Sushi Bar, Japanese
Average price: $11-30
Area: Brookline Village
Address: 238 Washington St
Brookline, MA 02445
Phone: (617) 734-6465

#464
UBurger
Category: Burgers
Average price: Under $10
Area: Allston/Brighton
Address: 1022 Commonwealth Ave
Boston, MA 02215
Phone: (617) 487-4855

#465
Omni Parker House
Category: Hotels, Breakfast & Brunch
Average price: $31-60
Area: Downtown
Address: 60 School St
Boston, MA 02108
Phone: (617) 227-8600

#466
Hot Pot Buffet
Category: Chinese, Buffets
Average price: $11-30
Area: Chinatown
Address: 70 Beach St
Boston, MA 02111
Phone: (617) 338-0808

#467
Sister Sorel
Category: Bar, American
Average price: $11-30
Area: South End
Address: 645 Tremont St
Boston, MA 02116
Phone: (617) 266-4600

#468
Smith & Wollensky
Category: Steakhouse
Average price: Above $61
Area: Waterfront, South Boston
Address: 294 Congress St
Boston, MA 02210
Phone: (617) 778-2200

#469
Tampopo
Category: Japanese
Average price: Under $10
Area: Porter Square
Address: 1815 Massachusetts Ave
Cambridge, MA 02140
Phone: (617) 868-5457

#470
T Anthony's Pizzeria & Restaurant
Category: Pizza, Italian
Average price: Under $10
Area: Allston/Brighton
Address: 1016 Commonwealth Ave
Boston, MA 02215
Phone: (617) 734-7708

#471
Bon Me
Category: Food Stands, Vietnamese
Average price: Under $10
Area: Downtown
Address: 602 Commonwealth Ave
Boston, MA 02215
Phone: (617) 945-2615

#472
Oliveiras Restaurant East Boston
Category: Brazilian, Barbeque
Average price: $11-30
Area: East Boston
Address: 297 Chelsea St
Boston, MA 02128
Phone: (617) 561-7277

#473
Stoli Bar & Restaurant
Category: Russian, Lounge
Average price: $31-60
Area: Brookline Village
Address: 213 Washington St
Brookline, MA 02445
Phone: (617) 731-5070

#474
Same Old Place
Category: Pizza
Average price: Under $10
Area: Jamaica Plain
Address: 662 Ctr St
Jamaica Plain, MA 02130
Phone: (617) 524-9461

#475
The Friendly Toast
Category: Breakfast & Brunch
Average price: $11-30
Area: Kendall Square/MIT
Address: 1 Kendall Sq
Cambridge, MA 02139
Phone: (617) 621-1200

#476
Café de Lulu
Category: Chinese
Average price: Under $10
Area: Chinatown
Address: 42 Beach St
Boston, MA 02111
Phone: (617) 391-0888

#477
Habanero Mexican Grill
Category: Mexican
Average price: Under $10
Area: Allston/Brighton
Address: 166 Brighton Ave
Boston, MA 02134
Phone: (617) 254-0299

#478
Beauty's
Category: Pizza
Average price: Under $10
Area: Kendall Square/MIT
Address: 228 Broadway
Cambridge, MA 02139
Phone: (617) 876-6969

#479
Beauty's
Category: Pizza
Average price: Under $10
Area: Kendall Square/MIT
Address: 228 Broadway
Cambridge, MA 02139
Phone: (617) 876-6969

#480
Pit Stop Barbeque
Category: Barbeque
Average price: $11-30
Area: Mattapan
Address: 888A Morton St
Dorchester, MA 02124
Phone: (617) 436-0485

#481
Grasshopper Cafe
Category: Sandwiches, Breakfast & Brunch
Average price: $11-30
Area: Charlestown
Address: 229-231 Bunker Hill St
Boston, MA 02129
Phone: (617) 242-0000

#482
Papagayo
Category: Mexican
Average price: $11-30
Area: Waterfront, South Boston
Address: 283 Summer St
Boston, MA 02210
Phone: (617) 423-1000

#483
Sweet Cheeks
Category: Southern, Bar
Average price: $11-30
Area: Fenway
Address: 1381 Boylston St
Boston, MA 02215
Phone: (617) 266-1300

#484
Moody's Falafel Palace
Category: Falafel
Average price: Under $10
Area: Central Square
Address: 25 Central Sq
Cambridge, MA 02139
Phone: (617) 864-0827

#485
Boston Chops
Category: Bar, Steakhouse
Average price: $31-60
Area: South End
Address: 1375 Washington St
Boston, MA 02118
Phone: (617) 227-5011

#486
Algiers Coffee House
Category: Coffee & Tea, Middle Eastern
Average price: $11-30
Area: Harvard Square
Address: 40 Brattle St
Cambridge, MA 02138
Phone: (617) 492-1557

#487
Ghazal Fine Indian Cuisine
Category: Indian
Average price: $11-30
Area: Jamaica Plain
Address: 711 Centre St
Boston, MA 02130
Phone: (617) 522-9500

#488
Uptown Cafe
Category: Italian, Sandwiches
Average price: Under $10
Area: Downtown, Beacon Hill
Address: 120 Cambridge St
Boston, MA 02114
Phone: (617) 227-1181

#489
The Middle East Restaurant And Nightclub
Category: Middle Eastern, Music Venue
Average price: $11-30
Area: Central Square
Address: 472 Massachusetts Ave
Cambridge, MA 02139
Phone: (617) 864-3278

#490
OTTO
Category: Pizza, Bar
Average price: $11-30
Area: Allston/Brighton
Address: 888 Commonwealth Ave
Boston, MA 02215
Phone: (617) 232-0447

#491
Boloco Copley Square
Category: American, Mexican
Average price: Under $10
Area: Back Bay
Address: 569 Boylston St
Boston, MA 02116
Phone: (617) 259-1619

#492
Sonsie
Category: American, Wine Bar
Average price: $31-60
Area: Back Bay
Address: 327 Newbury St
Boston, MA 02115
Phone: (617) 351-2500

#493
Jimmy's Steer House
Category: Steakhouse
Average price: $11-30
Area: Arlington Heights
Address: 1111 Massachusetts Ave
Arlington, MA 02476
Phone: (781) 646-4450

#494
Saloon
Category: American, Pub
Average price: $11-30
Area: Davis Square
Address: 255 Elm St
Somerville, MA 02144
Phone: (617) 628-4444

#495
Charlie's Kitchen
Category: American, Dive Bar
Average price: Under $10
Area: Harvard Square
Address: 10 Eliot St
Cambridge, MA 02138
Phone: (617) 492-9646

#496
Dim Sum Chef
Category: Dim Sum
Average price: Under $10
Area: Allston/Brighton
Address: 1095 Commonwealth Ave
Boston, MA 02215
Phone: (617) 254-2073

#497
Sabatino's Italian
Category: Italian, Pizza
Average price: Under $10
Area: Allston/Brighton
Address: 1443 Commonwealth Ave
Brighton, MA 02135
Phone: (617) 787-9393

#498
Yard House
Category: American, American
Average price: $11-30
Area: Fenway
Address: 126 Brookline Avenue
Boston, MA 02215
Phone: (617) 236-4083

#499
Petit Robert Bistro
Category: French
Average price: $11-30
Area: South End
Address: 480 Columbus Ave
Boston, MA 02118
Phone: (617) 867-0600

#500
Jamaica Plain House of Pizza
Category: Pizza, Italian
Average price: Under $10
Area: Jamaica Plain
Address: 775 Centre St
Jamaica Plain, MA 02130
Phone: (617) 522-4154

Made in the USA
Columbia, SC
22 December 2020